I0439669

Consumer Compliance (CC)

Privacy of Consumer Financial Information

October 2011

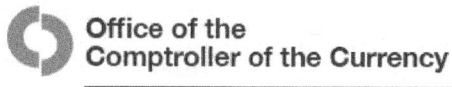

**Office of the
Comptroller of the Currency**

Washington, DC 20219

Privacy of Consumer Financial Information

Contents

Introduction

This booklet provides background information and optional expanded examination procedures for the consumer protection topics listed below.

Examiners will select which of these procedures are necessary, if any, after first completing a compliance core assessment as outlined in the OCC's "Large Bank Supervision" and "Community Bank Supervision" *Comptroller's Handbook* booklets.

Background and Summary

Title V, subtitle A of the Gramm–Leach–Bliley Act of 1999 (GLBA) governs the treatment of nonpublic personal information about consumers by financial institutions. Section 502 of the subtitle, subject to certain exceptions, prohibits a financial institution from disclosing nonpublic personal information about a consumer to nonaffiliated third parties, unless the institution satisfies various notice and opt-out requirements and provided that the consumer has not elected to opt out of the disclosure. Section 503 requires the institution to provide notice of its privacy policies and practices to its customers. Section 504 authorizes the issuance of regulations to implement these provisions.

In 2000, the financial institution regulatory agencies and the National Credit Union Administration (NCUA)[1] published regulations implementing provisions of the GLBA governing the treatment of nonpublic personal information about consumers by financial institutions. The regulations require financial institutions to provide particular notices and to comply with certain limitations on disclosure of nonpublic personal information, as summarized below (a more complete discussion appears later in this document):

- A financial institution must provide a notice of its privacy policies and practices with respect to both affiliated and nonaffiliated third parties, and allow the consumer to opt out of the disclosure of the consumer's

---

[1] The NCUA published its final rule in the *Federal Register* on May 18, 2000 (65 FR 31722). The Board of Governors of the Federal Reserve System, the Federal Deposit Insurance Corporation, the Office of the Comptroller of the Currency, and the Office of Thrift Supervision jointly published their final rules on June 1, 2000 (65 FR 35162).

nonpublic personal information to a nonaffiliated third party if the disclosure is outside of the exceptions in sections 13, 14, or 15 of the regulations.

- Regardless of whether a financial institution shares nonpublic personal information, the institution must provide notices of its privacy policies to its customers.
- A financial institution generally may not disclose customer account numbers to any nonaffiliated third party for marketing purposes.
- A financial institution must follow reuse and redisclosure limitations on any nonpublic personal information it receives from a nonaffiliated financial institution.

Section 728 of the Financial Services Regulatory Relief Act of 2006 required the agencies to develop a model privacy form on which financial institutions may rely as a "safe harbor" to provide disclosures under the privacy rules (See 15 USC 6803(e)).

On December 1, 2009, the four federal banking agencies and four additional federal regulatory agencies[2] jointly released a voluntary model privacy notice form designed to make it easier for consumers to understand how financial institutions collect and share nonpublic personal information. The final rule adopting the model form was effective on December 31, 2009, except that notices that were provided on or before December 31, 2010, using sample clauses contained in an appendix to the 2000 rule, continued to receive the safe harbor for compliance with the notice requirements of the regulation for one year. Appendix B, which now contains these sample clauses, is deleted from the agencies' rule effective January 1, 2012.

Effective July 21, 2011, the Dodd–Frank Wall Street Reform and Consumer Protection Act transfers responsibility for prescribing rules under the GLBA's privacy provisions to the Bureau of Consumer Financial Protection (CFPB) (See 12 USC 5512). The privacy rules discussed below will be published in Chapter X of Title 12 of the Code of Federal Regulations.

---

[2] 74 FR 62890 (December 1, 2009) The four additional federal regulators are the NCUA, the Commodity Futures Trading Commission, the Federal Trade Commission, and the Securities and Exchange Commission.

Definitions and Key Concepts

In discussing the duties and limitations imposed by the regulations, a number of key concepts are used. These concepts include financial institution, nonpublic personal information, nonaffiliated third party, the "opt-out" right and the exceptions to that right, and consumer and customer. Each concept is briefly discussed below. A more complete explanation of each appears in the regulations.

Financial institution: Any institution the business of which is engaging in activities that are financial in nature or incidental to such financial activities, as determined by section 4(k) of the Bank Holding Company Act of 1956 (See 12 USC 1843(k)). Financial institutions can include banks, securities brokers and dealers, insurance underwriters and agents, finance companies, and mortgage bankers[3]

Nonpublic personal information: Generally, any information that is not publicly available and that

- a consumer provides to a financial institution to obtain a financial product or service from the institution.
- results from a transaction between the consumer and the institution involving a financial product or service.
- a financial institution otherwise obtains about a consumer in connection with providing a financial product or service.

Information is publicly available if an institution has a reasonable basis to believe that the information is made available lawfully to the general public from government records, widely distributed media, or legally required disclosures to the general public. Examples include information in a published telephone book or a publicly recorded document, such as a mortgage or securities filing.

---

[3] Certain functionally regulated subsidiaries, such as brokers, dealers, and investment advisors, will be subject to privacy regulations issued by the Securities and Exchange Commission. Other functionally regulated subsidiaries, such as futures commission merchants, commodity trading advisors, commodity pool operators, and introducing brokers in commodities, are subject to privacy regulations issued by the Commodity Futures Trading Commission. Insurance entities may be subject to privacy regulations issued by their respective state insurance authorities.

Nonpublic personal information may include individual items of information as well as lists of information. For example, nonpublic personal information may include names, addresses, phone numbers, social security numbers, income, credit score, and information obtained through Internet collection devices such as cookies.

There are special rules regarding lists. Publicly available information would be treated as nonpublic if it were included on a list of consumers derived from nonpublic personal information. For example, a list of the names and addresses of a financial institution's depositors would be nonpublic personal information even though the names and addresses might be published in local telephone directories, because the list is derived from the fact that a person has a deposit account with an institution, which is not publicly available information.

However, if the financial institution has a reasonable basis to believe that certain customer relationships are a matter of public record, then any list of these relationships would be considered publicly available information. For instance, a list of mortgage customers whose mortgages are recorded in public records would be considered publicly available information. The institution could provide a list of such customers, and include on that list any other publicly available information it has about the customers on that list without having to provide notice or the opportunity to opt out (see below for definition).

Nonaffiliated third party: Any person except a financial institution's affiliate or a person employed jointly by a financial institution and a company that is not the institution's affiliate. An "affiliate" of a financial institution is any company that controls, is controlled by, or is under common control with the financial institution.

"Opt-out" right and the exceptions: Consumers must be given the right to "opt out" of, or prevent, a financial institution from disclosing nonpublic personal information about them to a nonaffiliated third party, unless an exception to that right applies. The exceptions are detailed in sections 13, 14, and 15 of the regulations and described below. As part of the opt-out right, consumers must be given a reasonable opportunity and a reasonable means to opt out. What constitutes a *reasonable opportunity to opt out* depends on the circumstances surrounding the consumer's transaction, but a consumer must be allowed a reasonable amount of time to exercise the opt-out right. For example, it would be reasonable if the financial institution allows 30 days from the date of mailing a notice or 30 days after customer acknowledgment of an electronic notice for an opt-out direction to be returned. What constitutes a *reasonable means to opt out* may include check-off boxes, a reply form, or a toll-free telephone number, again depending on the circumstances surrounding the consumer's transaction. It is not reasonable to require a consumer to write his or her own letter as the only means to opt out.

Exceptions to the opt-out right are summarized below and detailed in sections 13, 14, and 15 of the regulations. Financial institutions need not comply with opt-out requirements if they limit disclosure of nonpublic personal information. Exceptions include disclosure

- to a nonaffiliated third party to perform services for the financial institution or to function on its behalf, including marketing the institution's own products or services or those offered jointly by the institution and another financial institution. The exception is permitted only if the financial institution provides notice of these arrangements and by contract prohibits the third party from disclosing or using the information for other than the specified purposes. The contract for a joint marketing agreement must provide that the parties to the agreement are jointly offering, sponsoring, or endorsing a financial product or service. However, if the service or function is covered by the exceptions in section 14 or 15 (discussed below), the financial institution need not comply with the additional disclosure and confidentiality requirements of section 13. Disclosure under this exception could include the outsourcing of marketing to an advertising company (section 13).
- as necessary to effect, administer, or enforce a transaction that a consumer requests or authorizes, or under certain other circumstances relating to existing relationships with customers. Disclosures under this exception could be in connection with the audit of credit information, administration of a rewards program, or to provide an account statement (section 14).
- for specified other disclosures that a financial institution normally makes, such as to protect against or prevent actual or potential fraud; to the financial institution's attorneys, accountants, and auditors; or to comply with applicable legal requirements, such as the disclosure of information to regulators (section 15).

Consumer and customer: The distinction between consumers and customers is significant because financial institutions have additional disclosure duties regarding customers. All customers covered under the regulation are consumers, but not all consumers are customers.

Consumer: A person, or that person's legal representative, who obtains or has obtained a financial product or service from a financial institution that is to be used primarily for personal, family, or household purposes.

Financial service: Includes, among other things, a financial institution's evaluation or brokerage of information that the institution collects with a request or an application from a consumer for a financial product or service. For example, a financial service includes a lender's evaluation of an application for a consumer loan or for opening a deposit account even if the application is ultimately rejected or withdrawn.

A consumer who is not a customer is entitled to an initial privacy and opt-out notice only if his or her financial institution wants to share his or her nonpublic personal information with nonaffiliated third parties outside the exceptions.

Customer: A consumer who has a "customer relationship" with a financial institution. A customer relationship is a *continuing* relationship between a consumer and a financial institution under which the institution provides one or more financial products or services to the consumer that are to be used primarily for personal, family, or household purposes.

For example, a customer relationship may be established when a consumer engages in one of the following activities with a financial institution:

- Maintains a deposit or investment account
- Obtains a loan
- Enters into a lease of personal property
- Obtains financial, investment, or economic advisory services for a fee

Customers are entitled to initial and annual privacy notices regardless of the information disclosure practices of their financial institution.

There is a special rule for loans. When a financial institution sells the servicing rights to a loan to another financial institution, the customer relationship transfers with the servicing rights. However, any information on the borrower retained by the institution that sells the servicing rights must be accorded the protections due any consumer.

Note that isolated transactions alone will not cause a consumer to be treated as a customer. For example, if a person purchases a bank check from a financial institution where the person has no account, the person will be a consumer but not a customer of that institution because he or she has not established a customer relationship. Likewise, if a person uses the automated teller machine (ATM) of a financial institution where that person has no account, even repeatedly, the person will be a consumer, but not a customer of that institution.

Financial Institution Duties

The regulations establish specific duties and limitations for a financial institution based on its activities. Financial institutions that intend to disclose nonpublic personal information outside the exceptions will have to provide opt-out rights to their customers and to consumers who are not customers. All financial institutions have an obligation to provide an initial and annual notice of their privacy policies to their customers. All financial institutions must abide by the regulatory limits on the disclosure of account numbers to nonaffiliated third parties and on the redisclosure and reuse of nonpublic personal information received from nonaffiliated financial institutions.

A brief summary of financial institution duties and limitations follows. A more complete explanation of each appears in the regulations.

Notice and Opt-Out Duties to Consumers

If a financial institution intends to disclose nonpublic personal information about any of its consumers (whether or not they are customers) to a nonaffiliated third party, and an exception does not apply, then the financial institution must provide to the consumer all of the following:

- An initial notice of its privacy policies
- An opt-out notice (including, among other things, a reasonable means to opt out)
- A reasonable opportunity, before the financial institution discloses the information to the nonaffiliated third party, to opt out

The financial institution may not disclose any nonpublic personal information to nonaffiliated third parties, except under the enumerated exceptions *unless* these notices have been provided *and* the consumer has not opted out. Additionally, the institution must provide a *revised notice* before the financial institution begins to share a new category of nonpublic personal information or shares information with a new category of nonaffiliated third party in a manner that was not described in the previous notice.

Note that a financial institution need not comply with the initial and opt-out notice requirements for consumers who are not customers if the institution limits disclosure of nonpublic personal information to the exceptions.

Notice Duties to Customers

In addition to the duties described above, there are several duties unique to customers. In particular, regardless of whether a financial institution discloses or intends to disclose nonpublic personal information, the financial institution must provide notice to its customers of its privacy policies and practices at various times.

- A financial institution must provide an *initial notice* of its privacy policies and practices to each customer, not later than the time a customer relationship is established. Section 4(e) of the regulations describes the exceptional cases in which delivery of the notice is allowed subsequent to the establishment of the customer relationship.

- A financial institution must provide an *annual notice* at least once in any period of 12 consecutive months during the continuation of the customer relationship.
- Generally, new privacy notices are not required for each new product or service. However, a financial institution must provide a *new notice* to an existing customer when the customer obtains a new financial product or service from the institution, if the initial or annual notice most recently provided to the customer was *not* accurate for the new financial product or service.
- When a financial institution does not disclose nonpublic personal information (other than as permitted under the section 14 and section 15 exceptions) and does not reserve the right to do so, the institution has the option of providing a simplified notice.

Requirements for Notices

Clear and conspicuous. Privacy notices must be clear and conspicuous, meaning they must be reasonably understandable and designed to call attention to the nature and significance of the information contained in the notice. The regulations do not prescribe specific methods for making a notice clear and conspicuous, but do provide examples of ways in which to achieve the standard, such as the use of short explanatory sentences or bullet lists, and the use of plain-language headings and easily readable typeface and type size. Privacy notices also must accurately reflect the institution's privacy practices.

Delivery rules. Privacy notices must be provided so that each recipient can reasonably be expected to receive actual notice in writing, or if the consumer agrees, electronically. To meet this standard, a financial institution could, for example, (1) hand-deliver a printed copy of the notice to its consumers, (2) mail a printed copy of the notice to a consumer's last known address, or (3) for the consumer who conducts transactions electronically, post the notice on the institution's Internet Web site and require the consumer to acknowledge receipt of the notice as a necessary step to completing the transaction.

For customers only, a financial institution must provide the initial notice (as well as the annual notice and any revised notice) so that a customer may be able to retain or subsequently access the notice. A written notice satisfies this requirement. For customers who obtain financial products or services electronically and agree to receive their notices on the institution's Web site, the institution may provide the current version of its privacy notice on its Web site.

Notice content. A privacy notice must contain specific disclosures. However, a financial institution may provide to consumers who are not customers a "short form" initial notice, together with an opt-out notice, stating that the institution's privacy notice is available upon request, and explaining a reasonable means for the consumer to obtain it. The following is a list of disclosures regarding nonpublic personal information that institutions must provide in their privacy notices, as applicable:

- Categories of nonpublic information collected
- Categories of nonpublic information disclosed
- Categories of affiliates and nonaffiliated third parties to whom the institution may disclose information
- Policies with respect to the treatment of former customers' information.
- Information disclosed to service providers and joint marketers (section 13)
- An explanation of the opt-out right and methods for opting out
- Any opt-out notices the institution must provide under the Fair Credit Reporting Act with respect to affiliate information sharing
- Policies for protecting the security and confidentiality of information
- A statement that the institution makes disclosures to other nonaffiliated third parties as permitted by law (sections 14 and 15)

Model Privacy Notice Form. Appendix A to each federal banking agency's privacy regulation contains the model privacy notice form jointly issued in 2009. A financial institution can use the model form to obtain a safe harbor for compliance with the content requirements for notifying consumers of its information-sharing practices and their right to opt out of certain sharing practices. To obtain the safe harbor, the institution must provide a model form in accordance with the instructions set forth in appendix A of its regulatory agency's privacy regulation. The final rule adopting the model privacy form and accompanying safe harbor became effective on December 31, 2009, except that notices that were provided on or before December 31, 2010, using sample clauses contained in an appendix to the 2000 rule, continued to receive the safe harbor for compliance with the notice requirements of the regulation for one year. Appendix B, which now contains these sample clauses, is deleted from the agencies' rule effective January 1, 2012.

Limitations on Disclosure of Account Numbers

A financial institution must not disclose an account number or similar form of access number or access code for a credit card, deposit, or transaction account to any nonaffiliated third party (other than a consumer reporting agency) for use in telemarketing, direct mail marketing, or other marketing through electronic mail to the consumer.

The disclosure of encrypted account numbers without an accompanying means of decryption, however, is not subject to this prohibition. The regulation also expressly allows disclosures by a financial institution to its agent to market the institution's own products or services (although the financial institution must not authorize the agent to directly initiate charges to the customer's account). Also not barred are disclosures to participants in private-label or affinity card programs, when the participants are identified to the customer at the time the customer enters the program.

Redisclosure and Reuse Limitations on Nonpublic Personal Information Received

If a financial institution receives nonpublic personal information from a nonaffiliated financial institution, its disclosure and use of the information is limited.

- For nonpublic personal information received under a section 14 or 15 exception, the financial institution is limited to disclosing the information to
  - the affiliates of the financial institution from which it received the information.
  - its own affiliates, which may, in turn, disclose and use the information only to the extent that the financial institution may do so.

- use it pursuant to a section 14 or 15 exception (for example, an institution receiving information for account processing could disclose the information to its auditors).

- For nonpublic personal information received other than under a section 14 or 15 exception, the recipient's use of the information is unlimited, but its disclosure of the information is limited to disclosing the information to
  - the affiliates of the financial institution from which it received the information.
  - its own affiliates, which may, in turn, disclose the information only to the extent that the financial institution can do so.
  - any other person, if the disclosure would be lawful if made directly to that person by the financial institution from which it received the information. For example, an institution that received a customer list from another financial institution could disclose the list (1) in accordance with the privacy policy of the financial institution that provided the list, (2) subject to any opt-out election or revocation by the consumers on the list, and (3) in accordance with appropriate exceptions under sections 14 and 15.

Other Matters

Fair Credit Reporting Act

The regulations do not modify, limit, or supersede the operation of the Fair Credit Reporting Act.

State Law

The regulations do not supersede, alter, or affect any state statute, regulation, order, or interpretation, except to the extent that it is inconsistent with the regulations. A state statute, regulation, order, or interpretation is consistent with the regulations if the protection it affords any consumer is greater than the protection provided under the regulations, as determined by the CFPB.

Guidelines Regarding Protecting Customer Information

The regulations require a financial institution to disclose its policies and practices for protecting the confidentiality, security, and integrity of nonpublic personal information about consumers (whether or not they are customers). The disclosure need not describe these policies and practices in detail but instead may describe in general terms who is authorized to have access to the information and whether the institution has security practices and procedures in place to ensure the confidentiality of the information in accordance with the institution's policies.

The financial institution regulatory agencies published guidelines (See 12 CFR 30, Appendix B), pursuant to section 501(b) of the GLBA, that address steps that a financial institution should take to protect customer information. The guidelines relate only to information about customers, rather than all consumers. Compliance examiners should consider the findings of a 501(b) inspection during the compliance examination of a financial institution to evaluate the accuracy of the institution's disclosure regarding data security.

References

Laws

15 USC 6801-6809, Gramm–Leach–Bliley Act

Regulations

12 CFR 40, Privacy of consumer financial information

Expanded Procedures—Privacy of Consumer Financial Information

Objective: Determine the bank's level of compliance with the Privacy of Consumer Financial Information.

1. Assess the quality of a financial institution's compliance management policies and procedures for implementing the privacy regulation, specifically ensuring consistency between what the financial institution tells consumers in its notices about its policies and practices and what it actually does.

2. Determine a financial institution's compliance with the privacy regulation, specifically in meeting the following requirements, by completing the Privacy of Consumer Financial Information Worksheet:

    - Providing to customers notices of its privacy policies and practices that are timely, accurate, clear, and conspicuous, and that are delivered so that each customer can reasonably be expected to receive actual notice.
    - Disclosing nonpublic personal information to nonaffiliated third parties, other than under an exception, after first meeting the applicable requirements for giving consumers notice and the right to opt out.
    - Appropriately honoring consumer opt-out directions.
    - Lawfully using or disclosing nonpublic personal information received from a nonaffiliated financial institution.
    - Disclosing account numbers only according to the limits in the regulations.

Privacy of Consumer Financial Information Examination Worksheet

This worksheet can be used for reviewing audit work papers, evaluating bank policies, performing expanded procedures, and training, as appropriate. Complete only those sections of the worksheet that specifically relate to the issue being reviewed, evaluated, or tested, and retain those completed sections in the work papers.

When reviewing audit or evaluating bank policies, a "no" answer indicates a possible exception or deficiency and should be explained in the work papers. When performing expanded procedures, a "no" answer indicates a violation and should be explained in the work papers. If a line item is not applicable within the area you are reviewing, indicate "NA."

Privacy of Consumer Financial Information Examination Worksheet
Underline the applicable use:

Audit   Bank Policies   Expanded Procedures

Subpart A			
Initial Notice	**Yes**	**No**	**NA**
1. Does the institution provide a clear and conspicuous notice that accurately reflects its privacy policies and practices to *all customers* not later than when the customer relationship is established, other than as allowed in 12 CFR 40.(4)(e) (12 CFR 40.4(a)(1))? *Note:* No notice is required if nonpublic personal information is disclosed to nonaffiliated third parties only under an exception in sections 14 and 15, and there is no customer relationship (12 CFR 40.4(b)). With respect to credit relationships, an institution establishes a customer relationship when it originates a consumer loan. If the institution subsequently sells the servicing rights to the loan to another financial institution, the customer relationship transfers with the servicing rights (12 CFR 40.4(c)).			
2. Does the institution provide a clear and conspicuous notice that accurately reflects its privacy policies and practices to *all consumers* who are not customers before any nonpublic personal information about the consumer is disclosed to a nonaffiliated third party, other than under an exception in 12 CFR 40.14 or 15 (12 CFR 40.4(a)(2))?			

1. Does the institution provide to *existing customers* who obtain a new financial product or service an initial privacy notice that covers the customer's new financial product or service, if the most recent notice provided to the customer was not accurate with respect to the new financial product or service (12 CFR 40.4(d)(1))?			

4. Does the institution provide initial notice *after establishing a customer relationship* only:
 	
   a. If the customer relationship is not established at the customer's election (12 CFR 40.4(e)(1)(i))—or—
 	
   b. If to do otherwise would substantially delay the customer's transaction (e.g., in the case of a telephone application), and the customer agrees to the subsequent delivery (12 CFR 40.4 (e)(1)(ii))?			

5. When the subsequent delivery of a privacy notice is permitted, does the institution provide notice after establishing a customer relationship within a reasonable time (12 CFR 40.4(e))?			
Annual Privacy Notice			
6. Does the institution provide a clear and conspicuous notice that accurately reflects its privacy policies and practices at least annually (that is, at least once in any period of 12 consecutive months) to all customers, throughout the customer relationship (12 CFR 40.5(a)(1)and 40.(2))? **Note:** Annual notices are not required for former customers (12 CFR 40.5(b)(1)and (2)).			
7. Does the institution provide an annual privacy notice to each customer whose loan the institution owns the right to service (12 CFR 40.5(c), 4(c)(2))?			

Content of Privacy Notice			
Opt Out Notice			
8. If the institution discloses nonpublic personal information about a consumer to a nonaffiliated third party, and the exceptions under 12 CFR 40.13-40.15 do not apply, does the institution provide the consumer with a clear and conspicuous opt-out notice that accurately explains the right to opt out (12 CFR 40.7(a)(1))?			
9. Does the opt-out notice state: a. That the institution discloses or reserves the right to disclose nonpublic personal information about the consumer to a nonaffiliated third party (12 CFR 40.7(a)(1)(i))? b. That the consumer has the right to opt out of that disclosure (12 CFR 40.7(a)(1)(ii))? and c. A reasonable means by which the consumer may opt out (12 CFR 40.7(a)(1)(iii))?			
10. Does the institution provide the consumer with the following information about the right to opt out: a. All the categories of nonpublic personal information that the institution discloses or reserves the right to disclose (12 CFR 40.7(a)(2)(i)(A))? b. All the categories of nonaffiliated third parties to whom the information is disclosed (12 CFR 40.7(a)(2)(i)(A))?			
11. Does the institution provide the consumer with at least one of the following reasonable means of opting out, or with another reasonable means: a. Check-off boxes prominently displayed on the relevant forms with the opt-out notice (12 CFR 40.7(a)(2)(ii)(A))? b. A reply form included with the opt-out notice (12 CFR 40.7(a)(2)(ii)(B))? c. An electronic means to opt out, such as a form that can be sent via electronic mail or a process at the institution's Web site, if the consumer agrees to the electronic delivery of			

information (12 CFR 40.7(a)(2)(ii)(C))? or d. A toll-free telephone number (12 CFR 40.7(a)(2)(ii)(D))? **Note:** The institution may require the consumer to use one specific means, as long as that means is reasonable for that consumer (12 CFR 40.7(a)(iv)).			
12. If the institution delivers the opt-out notice after the initial notice, does the institution provide the initial notice once again with the opt-out notice (12 CFR 40.7(c))?			
13. Does the institution provide an opt-out notice, explaining how the institution will treat opt-out directions by the joint consumers, to at least one party in a joint consumer relationship (12 CFR 40.7(d)(1))?			
14. Does the institution permit each of the joint consumers in a joint relationship to opt out (12 CFR 40.7(d)(2))?			
15. Does the opt-out notice to joint consumers state that either: a. The institution will consider an opt out by a joint consumer as applying to all associated joint consumers (12 CFR 40.7(d)(2)(i))? or b. Each joint consumer is permitted to opt out separately (12 CFR 40.7(d)(2)(ii))?			
16. If each joint consumer may opt out separately, does the institution permit: a. One joint consumer to opt out on behalf of all of the joint consumers (12 CFR 40.7(d)(3))? b. The joint consumers to notify the institution in a single response (12 CFR 40.7(d)(5))? c. Each joint consumer to opt out either for himself or herself, and/or for another joint consumer (12 CFR 40.7(d)(5))?			
17. Does the institution refrain from requiring all joint consumers to opt out before implementing any opt-out direction with respect to the joint account (12 CFR 40.7(d)(4))?			

18. Does the institution comply with a consumer's direction to opt out as soon as is reasonably practicable after receiving it (12 CFR 40.7(e))?			
19. Does the institution allow the consumer to opt out at any time (12 CFR 40.7(f))?			
20. Does the institution continue to honor the consumer's opt-out direction until revoked by the consumer in writing, or, if the consumer agrees, electronically (12 CFR 40.7(g)(1))?			
21. When a customer relationship ends, does the institution continue to apply the customer's opt-out direction to the nonpublic personal information collected during, or related to, that specific customer relationship (but not to new relationships, if any, subsequently established by that customer) (12 CFR 40.7(g)(2))?			
Revised Notices			
22. Except as permitted by 12 CFR 40.13-40.15, does the institution refrain from disclosing any nonpublic personal information about a consumer to a nonaffiliated third party, other than as described in the initial privacy notice provided to the consumer, unless: a. The institution has provided the consumer with a clear and conspicuous revised notice that accurately describes the institution's privacy policies and practices (12 CFR 40.8(a)(1))? b. The institution has provided the consumer with a new opt-out notice (12 CFR 40.8(a)(2))? c, The institution has given the consumer a reasonable opportunity to opt out of the disclosure, before disclosing any information (12 CFR 40.8(a)(3))? d. The consumer has not opted out (12 CFR 40.8(a)(4))?			
23. Does the institution deliver a revised privacy notice when it: a. Discloses a new category of nonpublic personal information to a nonaffiliated third party (12 CFR 40.8(b)(1)(i))? b. Discloses nonpublic personal information to a new category of nonaffiliated third party (12 CFR 40.8(b)(1)(ii))?			

c. Discloses nonpublic personal information about a former customer to a nonaffiliated third party, if that former customer has not had the opportunity to exercise an opt-out right regarding that disclosure (12 CFR 40.8(b)(1)(iii))? *Note:* A revised notice is not required if the institution adequately described the nonaffiliated third party or information to be disclosed in the prior privacy notice (12 CFR 40.8(b)(2)).			
Delivery Methods			
24. Does the institution deliver the privacy and opt-out notices, including the short-form notice, so that the consumer can reasonably be expected to receive actual notice in writing or, if the consumer agrees, electronically (12 CFR 40.9(a))?			
25. Does the institution use a reasonable means for delivering the notices, such as: a. Hand-delivery of a printed copy (12 CFR 40.9(b)(1)(i))? b. Mailing a printed copy to the last known address of the consumer (12 CFR 40.9(b)(1)(ii))? c. For the consumer who conducts transactions electronically, clearly and conspicuously posting the notice on the institution's electronic site and requiring the consumer to acknowledge receipt as a necessary step to obtaining a financial product or service (12 CFR 40.9(b)(1)(iii))? d. For isolated transactions, such as ATM transactions, posting the notice on the screen and requiring the consumer to acknowledge receipt as a necessary step to obtaining the financial product or service (12 CFR 40.9(b)(1)(iv))? *Note:* Insufficient or unreasonable means of delivery include: exclusively oral notice, in person or by telephone, branch or office signs or generally published advertisements, and electronic mail to a customer who does not obtain products or services electronically (12 CFR 40.9 (b)(2)(i) and (ii), and (d)).			

26. For annual notices only, if the institution does not employ one of the methods described in question 36, does the institution employ one of the following reasonable means of delivering the notice such as: a. For the customer who uses the institution's Web site to access products and services electronically and who agrees to receive notices at the Web site, continuously posting the current privacy notice on the Web site in a clear and conspicuous manner (12 CFR 40.9(c)(1))? b. For the customer who has requested the institution refrain from sending any information about the customer relationship, making copies of the current privacy notice available upon customer request (12 CFR 40.9(c)(2))?			
27. For customers only, does the institution ensure that the initial, annual, and revised notices may be retained or obtained later by the customer in writing, or if the customer agrees, electronically (12 CFR 40.9(e)(1))?			
28. Does the institution use an appropriate means to ensure that notices may be retained or obtained later, such as: a. Hand-delivering of a printed copy of the notice (12 CFR 40.9(e)(2)(i))? b. Mailing a printed copy to the last known address of the customer (12 CFR 40.9(e)(2)(ii))? or c. Making the current privacy notice available on the institution's Web site (or via a link to the notice at another site) for the customer who agrees to receive the notice at the Web site (12 CFR 40.9(e)(2)(iii))?			
29. Does the institution provide at least one initial, annual, and revised notice, as applicable, to joint consumers (12 CFR 40.9(g))?			
Subpart B			
Limits on Disclosures to Nonaffiliated Third Parties			
30. Does the institution refrain from disclosing any nonpublic personal information about a consumer to a nonaffiliated third party, other than as permitted under 12 CFR 40.13-40.15, unless:			

a. It has provided the consumer with an initial notice (12 CFR 40.10(a)(1)(i))?			
b. It has provided the consumer with an opt-out notice (12 CFR 40.10(a)(1)(ii))?			
c. It has given the consumer a reasonable opportunity to opt out before the disclosure (12 CFR 40.10(a)(1)(iii))?			
d. The consumer has not opted out (12 CFR 40.10(a)(1)(iv))?			
Note: This disclosure limitation applies to consumers as well as to customers (12 CFR 40.10(b)(1)), and to all nonpublic personal information regardless of whether collected before or after receiving an opt-out direction (12 CFR 40.10(b)(2)).			
31. Does the institution provide the consumer with a reasonable opportunity to opt out such as by: a. Mailing the notices required by 12 CFR 40.10 and allowing the consumer to respond by toll-free telephone number, return mail, or other reasonable means (see question 22) within 30 days from the date mailed (12 CFR 40.10(a)(3)(i))? b. Where the consumer opens an online account with the institution and agrees to receive the notices required by 12 CFR 40.10 electronically, allowing the consumer to opt out by any reasonable means (see question 22) within 30 days from consumer acknowledgement of receipt of the notice in conjunction with opening the account (12 CFR 40.10(a)(3)(ii))? c. For isolated transactions, providing the notices required by 12 CFR 40.10 at the time of the transaction and requesting that the consumer decide, as a necessary part of the transaction, whether to opt out before the completion of the transaction (12 CFR 40.10(a)(3)(iii))?			
32. Does the institution allow the consumer to select certain nonpublic personal information or certain nonaffiliated third parties with respect to which the consumer wishes to opt out (12 CFR 40.10(c))? *Note:* An institution may allow partial opt outs in addition to, but may not allow them instead of, a comprehensive opt out.			

Limits on Redisclosure and Reuse of Information			
33. If the institution receives information from a nonaffiliated financial institution under an exception in 12 CFR 40.14 or 40.15, does the institution refrain from using or disclosing the information except: a. To disclose the information to the affiliates of the financial institution from which it received the information (12 CFR 40.11(a)(1)(i))? b. To disclose the information to its own affiliates, which are in turn limited by the same disclosure and use restrictions as the recipient institution (12 CFR 40.11(a)(1)(ii))? c. To disclose and use the information pursuant to an exception in 12 CFR 40.14 or 40.15 in the ordinary course of business to carry out the activity covered by the exception under which the information was received (12 CFR 40.11(a)(1)(iii))? *Note:* The disclosure or use described in item c of this question need not be directly related to the activity covered by the applicable exception. For instance, an institution receiving information for fraud-prevention purposes could provide the information to its auditors. But "in the ordinary course of business" does not include marketing (12 CFR 40.11(a)(2)).			
34. If the institution receives information from a nonaffiliated financial institution other than under an exception in 12 CFR 40.14 or 40.15, does the institution refrain from disclosing the information except: a. To the affiliates of the financial institution from which it received the information (12 CFR 40.11(b)(1)(i))? b. To its own affiliates, which are in turn limited by the same disclosure restrictions as the recipient institution (12 CFR 40.11(b)(1)(ii))? and c. To any other person, if the disclosure would be lawful if made directly to that person by the institution from which the recipient institution received the information (12 CFR 40.11(b)(1)(iii))?			

Limits on Sharing Account Number Information for Marketing Purposes			
35. Does the institution refrain from disclosing, directly or through affiliates, account numbers or similar forms of access numbers or access codes for a consumer's credit card account, deposit account, or transaction account to any nonaffiliated third party (other than a consumer reporting agency) for telemarketing, direct mail, or electronic mail marketing to the consumer, except: a. To the institution's agents or service providers solely to market the institution's own products or services, as long as the agent or service provider is not authorized to directly initiate charges to the account (12 CFR 40.12(b)(1))? or b. To a participant in a private label credit card program or an affinity or similar program where the participants in the program are identified to the customer when the customer enters into the program (12 CFR 40.12(b)(2))? *Note:* "Account numbers or similar forms of access numbers or access codes" do not include numbers in encrypted form, so long as the institution does not provide the recipient with a means of decryption (12 CFR 40.12(c)(1)). A transaction account does not include an account to which third parties cannot initiate charges (12 CFR 40.12(c)(2)).			
Subpart C			
Exception to Opt-Out Requirements for Service Providers and Joint Marketing			
36. If the institution discloses nonpublic personal information to a nonaffiliated third party without permitting the consumer to opt out, do the opt-out requirements of 12 CFR 40.7 and 40.10, and the revised notice requirements in 40.8, not apply because: a. The institution disclosed the information to a nonaffiliated third party who performs services for or functions on behalf of the institution (including joint marketing of financial products and services offered pursuant to a joint agreement as defined in 12 CFR 40.13 (b) (12 CFR 40.13(a)(1))? b. The institution has provided consumers with the initial notice (12 CFR 40.13(a)(1)(i))? c. The institution has entered into a contract with that party prohibiting the party from disclosing or using the information except to carry out the purposes for which the information			

Comptroller's Handbook   25   Privacy of Consumer Financial Information

was disclosed, including use under an exception in 12 CFR 40.14 or 40.15 in the ordinary course of business to carry out those purposes (12 CFR 40.13(a)(1)(ii))?			

Exceptions to Notice and Opt-Out Requirements for Processing and Servicing Transactions

27. If the institution discloses nonpublic personal information to nonaffiliated third parties, do the requirements for initial notice in 12 CFR 40.4(a)(2), opt-out in 12 CFR 40.7 and 40.10, revised notice in 40.8, and for service providers and joint marketing in 40.13 not apply because the information is disclosed as necessary to effect, administer, or enforce a transaction that the consumer requests or authorizes, or in connection with: a. Servicing or processing a financial product or service requested or authorized by the consumer (12 CFR 40.14(a)(1))? b. Maintaining or servicing the consumer's account with the institution or with another entity as part of a private-label credit card program or other credit extension on behalf of the entity (12 CFR 40.14(a)(2))? c. A proposed or actual securitization, secondary market sale (including sale of servicing rights) or other similar transaction related to a transaction of the consumer (12 CFR 40.14(a)(3))?			

38. If the institution uses a section 14 exception as necessary to effect, administer, or enforce a transaction, is it:
 	
a. Required, or is one of the lawful or appropriate methods to enforce the rights of the institution or other persons engaged in carrying out the transaction or providing the product or service (12 CFR 40.14(b)(1))
 	
b. Required, or is a usual, appropriate, or acceptable method to: (12 CFR 40.14(b)(2))
 	
    i. Carry out the transaction or the product or service business of which the transaction is a part, including recording, servicing, or maintaining the consumer's account in the ordinary course of business (12 CFR 40.14(b)(2)(i))?
 	
    ii. Administer or service benefits or claims? (12 CFR 40.14(b)(2)(ii))			

iii. Confirm or provide a statement or other record of the transaction or information on the status or value of the financial service or financial product to the consumer or the consumer's agent or broker? (12 CFR 40.14(b)(2)(iii))			
iv. Accrue or recognize incentives or bonuses? (12 CFR 40.14(b)(2)(iv))			
v. Underwrite insurance or for reinsurance or for certain other purposes related to a consumer's insurance? (12 CFR 40.14(b)(2)(v)) or			
vi. in connection with:			
(1) The authorizing, settling, billing, processing, clearing, transferring, reconciling, or collecting of amounts charged, debited, or otherwise paid by using a debit, credit, or other payment card, check, or account number, or by other payment means? (12 CFR 40.14(b)(2)(vi)(A))			
(2) The transfer of receivables, accounts, or interests therein (12 CFR 40.14(b)(2)(vi)(B))? or			
(3) The audit of debit, credit, or other payment information (12 CFR 40.14(b)(2)(vi)(C))?			
39. If the institution discloses nonpublic personal information to nonaffiliated third parties, do the requirements for initial notice in 12 CFR 40.4(a)(2), opt out in 40.7 and 40.10, revised notice in 40.8, and for service providers and joint marketers in 40.13, not apply because the institution makes the disclosure:			
a. With the consent or at the direction of the consumer (12 CFR 40.15(a)(1))?			
b. i. To protect the confidentiality or security of records (12 CFR 40.15(a)(2)(i))?			
ii. To protect against or prevent actual or potential fraud, unauthorized transactions, claims, or other liability (12 CFR 40.15(a)(2)(ii))?			
iii. For required institutional risk control or for resolving consumer disputes or inquiries? (12 CFR 40.15(a)(2)(iii))?			
iv. To persons holding a legal or beneficial interest relating to			

the consumer (12 CFR 40.15(a)(2)(iv))?—or—			
v. To persons acting in a fiduciary or representative capacity on behalf of the consumer (12 CFR 40.15(a)(2)(v))?			
c. To insurance rate advisory organizations, guaranty funds or agencies, agencies rating the institution, persons assessing compliance, and the institution's attorneys, accountants, and auditors (12 CFR 40.15(a)(3))?			
d. In compliance with the Right to Financial Privacy Act, or to law enforcement agencies (12 CFR 40.15(a)(4))?			
e. To a consumer reporting agency in accordance with the Fair Credit Reporting Act or from a consumer report reported by a consumer reporting agency (12 CFR 40.15(a)(5))?			
f. In connection with a proposed or actual sale, merger, transfer, or exchange of all or a portion of a business or operating unit, if the disclosure of nonpublic personal information concerns solely consumers of such business or unit (12 CFR 40.15(a)(6))?			
g. To comply with federal, state, or local laws, rules, or legal requirements (12 CFR 40.15(a)(7)(i))?			
h. To comply with a properly authorized civil, criminal, or regulatory investigation, or subpoena or summons by federal, state, or local authorities (12 CFR 40.15(a)(7)(ii))?			
i. To respond to judicial process or government regulatory authorities having jurisdiction over the institution for examination, compliance, or other purposes as authorized by law (12 CFR 40.15(a)(7)(iii))?			
Note: The regulation gives the following as an example of the exception described in item a of this question: "A consumer may specifically consent to (an institution's) disclosure to a nonaffiliated insurance company of the fact that the consumer has applied to (the institution) for a mortgage so that the insurance company can offer homeowner's insurance to the consumer."